# THE LOVE OF JESUS
## TO PENTITENTS

# The Love of Jesus to Pentitents

## Henry Edward Cardinal Manning

STABAT MATER PRESS

Published by Stabat Mater Press
www.stabatmaterpress.com

Cover design and interior typesetting by Stabat Mater Press. All artwork not cited is in the public domain.
Printed in the United States of America

ISBN (Paperback): 979-8-9997560-4-6

# Contents

# Foreword

ALBERT P. HOLDEN

The promise which Christ makes to His Apostles in Saint Matthew's gospel is fulfilled by Him when, after the Resurrection he miraculously appeared to them and said, "Peace be to you. As the Father hath sent Me, I also send you." When He had said this, He breathed on them and said to them, "Receive ye the Holy Ghost; whose sins you shall forgive, they are forgiven them; and whose sins you shall retain, they are retained." (John 20:21-23)

In this most solemn way, Christ bestows on His Apostles the power to forgive sins. A power which He had previously promised to them. Henceforth they are to be His ambassadors in the world. From the context is seen that Christ sent them to forgive sins in the same way in which He had been sent by His Heavenly Father, and not in a restricted sense.

## THIS POWER IMPLIES CONFESSION

Christ, during His lifetime, required two conditions for the forgiveness of sins. First, sorrow and secondly a firm purpose of amendment. Being God, He could read the hearts and thoughts of men, and consequently knew without being told what sins they had committed. With the Apostles, however, the case is different. They were not divine, but were ordinary men like ourselves. It was not in their power, except in special cases. to know the thoughts and read the hearts of men. Yet Christ had made them supreme judges in the spiritual world, with the power to give or withhold forgiveness. As in civil law a judge requires to have full knowledge of a case before passing judgment, so too in the case of sin, a transgression of the law of God. It was necessary for the Apostles to know the facts of each case before they could exercise their power as judge. What other way, since they could not read men's thoughts, is there by that the person wishing to have his sins forgiven should tell them to the Apostles?

Therefore, it follows that the means established by Christ for the forgiveness of sin entails three conditions:

1. Sorrow

2. A firm purpose of amendment

3. The telling (confessing) of sins to those to whom Christ said, "Whose sins you shall forgive, they are forgiven them."

## THIS POWER WAS MEANT FOR ALL TIME

The power of forgiving sins was not given to the Apostles alone, but to their lawful successors. Christ knew that the Apostles, being human, would one day die, but the Society which He had founded was to exist until the end of time. Observe the solemn words of Christ –

"As the Father hath sent me, so also do I send you."

He sent them clothed with His own power and He had commanded them to go into the whole world, to all nations, even to the consummation of the world. It was manifestly impossible for the Apostles themselves to go into the world and to every nation. Likewise, since they were human they could not exist until the consummation of the world, and yet Christ had promised to be with His Church to the end of time.

From the very nature and purpose of the Church it is plain that the power to forgive sins was not merely a personal prerogative of the Apostles but was granted to them in their official capacity and hence intended, like the Church, to be a permanent institution. The Church, with her divine mission, her apostolic succession, and her infallible teaching authority is destined to endure for all time. The power to forgive sins must be available and exercised as long as they are sinners and that means to the end of time. Any church not claiming to have this power could not possibly call itself the true Church of Christ.

As long, therefore, as the world shall last (even to the consummation of the world), shall the power to forgive sins, as instituted by Christ, exist and be exercised.

## WHERE IS THAT POWER TODAY?

So far it has been seen that Christ Himself forgave sins, that He bestowed this power on the Apostles and their successors and that the means established for the forgiveness of sins entails three conditions on the part of the penitent –

1. Sorrow

2. A firm purpose of amendment

3. The Confession of sins to one to whom Christ said, "Whose sins you shall forgive, they are forgiven them."

It is an obvious fact that there is sin in the world today. If there is sin, then there is sin to be forgiven. Where then can be found in the world today the means laid down by Christ and fulfilling the three conditions which He deemed necessary for the forgiveness of sins?

The answer to this question is – 'In the Catholic Confessional.' A Catholic goes to confession because he realizes that sin is an offence against God, depriving him of His friendship. Realizing this, he is truly sorry. Thus he fulfills the first condition laid down by Christ. His sorrow being sincere, he makes the resolution never wilfully to commit sin again. Thus is fulfilled the second condition, viz., the firm purpose of amendment. Going to confession, he humbly tells his sins to the priest because he recognizes that to the priest has been transmitted that power of remission given by Christ to His Apostles when He said to them, "Whose sins you shall forgive, they are forgiven them." He knows that the priest cannot possibly forgive sins of his own powers, for since sin is an offense against god, He alone can forgive it; but the priest is exercising that power which has been bestowed on him by God Himself. He is acting as the ambassador of Christ.

Thus in the confessional, or to give it its correct title, *the Sacrament of Penance*, is to be found a means for the forgiveness of sins which is identical with that established by Christ.

## HISTORICAL PROOF FOR CONFESSION

Even though some critics of the Catholic system will not go so far as to deny that Christ gave the power to forgive sins to His Apostles, yet they urge that the *confessing* of sins is a modern invention of the Church. A glance at the writings of the Fathers of the early Church is sufficient to disprove this objection, and show that this practice has been the custom from the time of the Apostles.

Saint Cyprian (died in 258): I entreat you, brethren, that each one should confess his own sins while he who has sinned is still in the flesh, while his confession may be received, while his satisfaction and the absolution given by the priest are still pleasing to the Lord. (De lapsis 28-29)

Origen (died 254): The layman who falls into sin cannot by himself wash away his own fault; he must have recourse to the Levite; he needs the priest nay at times he applies to one even greater than they; he needs even the Pontiff's help that he may obtain the remission of his sins. (In numeros x. 1.)

Saint Pacian (died 390): admonishes sinners "to cease to hide their wounded conscience" and to follow the example of "the sick who do not fear the Physician though he cut and burn the secret parts of the body"; he goes on to say, "'God alone' you say 'can remit sins.' Quite correct. But what he does through His priest, is done by His power." (Libellus ad pen. 6-8)

Saint Ambrose (died 397): Sins are forgiven through the Holy Ghost. Certainly, but men lend him their ministry...they forgive sins, not in their own name, but in the name of the Father, the Son and the Holy Ghost. (De Spiritu Sancto III, 137)

These history quotations have been confined to the early centuries because in later years they are more abundant, and the object of the ones quoted is achieved when it is shown that auricular confession was the practice of the infant Church, a practice obviously derived from the Apostles themselves.

It is worthy of note that until the time of the so-called reformation, no one ever questioned the right of the Church to forgive sins. The Montanists in the second century were declared heretics because they asserted that there were certain sins which the Church could not forgive, whilst the Carthari and Waldensians erred with regard to who could exercise the power of forgiveness. None of them contested the power of forgiving sins in the Church. Even in Luther's "Little Catechism" and the Apologia of the Augsburg Confession, Penance is mentioned as the third sacrament.

Again, all the Eastern sects have confession, i.e., the Sacrament of Penance, even though they separated from the Church at an early period in her history. This proves that at the time of their separation they practiced the Sacrament of Penance.

For one moment, suppose that Confession had not been the practice of the Catholic Church, and then the Pope of one of the councils had decided to impose on the faithful the obligation of confessing their sins. Obviously such a burden, distasteful to human nature, could not have been imposed without creating a vast upheaval. There would have been schisms and revolts everywhere, and the date of its institution would have stood out as definitely as that of any great event in history. But there is no trace in the history of the Church of any such happening. The absence of all protests during the centuries prior to the reformation is an evidence proof that Confession was regarded as a sacred duty imposed by none other than Christ Himself.

## THE VALUE OF CONFESSION

A glance at the alarming growth in the number of suicides in Europe since the reformation points to the salutary effects of Confession. It is an established fact that suicide has been much more common in non-Catholic that in Catholic communities. A writer in the Encyclopedia Britannica, in an article on 'Suicide' bears out this statement. In England and Wales during the years 1861 to 1906 the average annual number of suicides has gone on steadily increasing from 65 to 100 for every million inhabitants.

Are there not good grounds to assert that this terrible increase in self-destruction is due tot he far-reaching effect of the abolition of the Catholic Confessional? Nothing inclines a soul more to despair and eventually to self-destruction than does worry and sin. The Catholic, burdened maybe under all the troubles, worries and sins in the world, can go to confession and tell them to the priest. Perhaps he has never seen the priest before, perhaps he will never see him again. There is no danger of anything he has told the priest becoming known. He knows that the priest is bound under the 'Seal of Confession' never to reveal anything that has been told to him during the exercise of that divine office.

Above all, the Catholic knows that in confessing to the priest he is laying this troubles and sins before one who is not only a Judge but also a Physician. One who will not only, in the name of Christ, grant him forgiveness of his sins, but at the same time show him the particular remedy he needs.

Before the reformation suicides were rare when compared with their enormity today, and it was not until the time of the reformation that confession was abolished.

Hope has always been sanity, whereas despair is madness and folly. Christ came into the world to bring a message of hope. His teachings were the longed for 'Good Tidings,' and the Sacrament of Penance, as He instituted it, is a sacrament of Hope. It is a breakwater which reduces to a minimum the sea of despair which is engulfing the world today.

# Preface

*To the Very Reverend Robert Aston Coffin, Vice-Provincial of the Congregation of the Most Holy Redeemer.*

My dear Father Coffin,

The following pages, if they serve no other purpose, will at least convey to you my loving veneration for Saint Alphonsus and my affectionate attachment to his sons. To Saint Alphonsus, more than to any other Saint of these later times, is due the glory of having made the Sacrament of Penance sweet to Penitents. He was wont to say, against the rigorism of those who made the way of absolution difficult, "O, poor Blood of Jesus Christ!" and these great words contain a whole treatise of theology. They are a warning to the Priest to be generous of that which was given to the last drop so freely for our salvation, and to the Penitent to be generous in the use of the liberty which that most Precious Blood has purchased for us.

It was on one of those peaceful Feasts of Saint Alphonsus, in your church and garden at Saint Mary's, that the outline of the following thoughts came upon me with a new distinctness, and what I then said briefly at your bidding, I have here endeavoured to enlarge. But adequately to represent the Sacrament of Penance as an object of love, would need not only more than all I have written, but more than all I could write. Nevertheless, such as it is, accept it as a token of love to your Patron and to yourself, and pray that our dear Lord, who with clay can open the eyes of the blind, may use it for the light and healing of at least one soul. Commending myself to your prayers and to the intercession of Saint Alphonsus,

Believe me,
My dear Father Coffin,
Always affectionately yours,

HENRY E. MANNING.
Rome, Holy Week, 1862

# CHAPTER ONE

# The Sacrament of Penance

## SPECIAL SACRAMENT OF JESUS' COMPASSION

My object in the following pages is to speak of the Sacrament of Penance, not so much as it is divinely proposed to us through the Church as an object of our Faith, but as it is, an object of our love. I may, therefore, pass over as already known its Divine institution, its form, its matter, and its effects, to use the language of our Theology, and speak of it as it manifests to us the special tenderness of the love of Jesus, and draws us to itself by the effusion of special gifts of grace. The Sacrament of Penance is loved by Catholics, and hated by the world.

Like the Pillar, which of old guided the people of God, to us it is all light; to the world it is all darkness. There are two things of which the world would fain rid itself – of the day of judgment and the Sacrament of Penance: of the former, because it is searching and inevitable; of the latter, because it is the anticipation and the witness of judgment to come. For this cause there is no evil that the world will not say of the Confessional. It would dethrone the Eternal Judge if it could, therefore it spurns at the judge who sits in the tribunal of Penance, because he is within the reach of its heel. And not only the world without the Church, but the world within its unity, the impure, the false, the proud, the lukewarm, the worldly Catholic, and in a word, all who are impenitent, both fear and shrink from the shadow of the Great White Throne which falls upon them from the Sacrament of Penance. But to all who are penitent, in whatsoever degree and of whatsoever character, it is an object of love next after the Holy Eucharist, and for reasons which even the Blessed Sacrament of the altar does not equally present. The presence of Jesus in the Holy Eucharist is real and substantial, proper and personal, in all the fullness of His Godhead and Manhood. His presence in the Sacrament of Penance is by representation and by grace. In this then there is no comparison possible. In the Holy Eucharist Jesus manifests himself in His royalty, power, and glory.

In the Sacrament of Penance, in His tenderness as a Physician, and His compassion as the Good Shepherd. In the former He attracts and transforms us chiefly by His divine attributes: in the latter by His human experience, sympathy, and pity. In the Holy Eucharist Jesus draws us upwards to Himself: in the Sacrament of Penance He stoops down to listen to us and to open to us His Sacred Heart in the midst of our sins and in the hour of our greatest miseries The Holy Eucharist is Jesus reigning amongst the just; the Sacrament of Penance is Jesus seeking among sinners for those that are lost; the former is the Sacrament of Saints, the latter, of the sinful; and therefore to such as we are it comes down with a singular nearness, an intimate contact with our needs, and an articulate and human voice of help and solace. What, then, I would wish to do is to set down some of the reasons why we ought to contemplate and to approach it with love. The reasons I will give shall be as follows:

Because, first, it is the special Sacrament of the Compassion of Jesus; secondly, it is the means of self-knowledge; thirdly, of perfect contrition; fourthly, of reparation; and lastly, of perseverance.

1. And first, I would show that it is the special Sacrament of the Compassion of Jesus. The Sacrament of Penance then both manifests and applies the fulness of the grace of Jesus to sinners. When our Divine Lord breathed upon the Apostles and said, "Receive ye the Holy Ghost; whose sins you shall forgive they are forgiven, and whose sins you shall retain they are retained," (John 20:22-23) He exempted no soul then living, nor any who should afterwards come into the world, from this divine commission of pardon. He placed in the hands of His apostles the gift of His most Precious Blood, wherewith to sprinkle the whole earth and the people of all ages and generations. It was a commission to Jew and Gentile, to those who then believed, and to all who through their word should afterwards believe in His name. It included also the greatest of sinners. No man was shut out from the great mission of penance and of pardon. The oldest and most inveterate sinner, whose sin was red as scarlet and black as the night, the most proudly impious, and the most habitual in relapse, all are within the terms and reach of absolution. He has Himself said, "Every sin and blasphemy shall be forgiven men

save only one, the blasphemy of the Spirit shall not be forgiven," (Matthew 12:31) because the blasphemy of the Spirit is essentially a sin that is not repented of. It consists in blaspheming and rejecting the Lord of repentance and the very commission of forgiveness. It becomes unpardonable, not by a decree of the Divine legislation, but by the moral bar put by the sinner himself. This alone excepted, there is no sin of the flesh or spirit, howsoever inveterate, guilty, or aggravated, for which there is not a full, a perfect, and instant absolution.

But the Sacrament of Penance not only conveys pardon to all and for all sins whatsoever, it also bestows upon the soul an exuberance of divine gifts. As Baptism is our first spiritual resurrection, so, if we afterwards fall into mortal sin, Penance is our second. And therefore they are called the Sacraments of the dead, because they raise souls dead in sin to the life of justice, and in raising the soul they fill it with grace and charity. The sanctifying grace lost after Baptism is restored in penance, and not only so, but all the works of piety and charity, which through our mortal sins are mortified and die, by absolution are fully revived and live again before God.

Like as spring comes after winter and revives all things, and the lands and the woods, which a little while ago seemed dead, put on a new vigour and fruitfulness, so with the soul. It was dead, it is alive again, and all the fruits which hung withered on the bough are quickened once more with a new life. By Baptism we were sons of God, by sin we lost our adoption and fell from grace and charity; by Penance we are brought back again to Friendship and Sonship with our Father in Heaven. Such is the fulness of grace of which the Sacrament of Penance is a permanent and inexhaustible source.

2. Another way in which the Sacrament of Penance manifests the compassion of Jesus Christ is its freeness. This full, perfect, and universal absolution from all sins of our whole life in all their multitude and in all their guilt would be cheaply purchased by years of sorrow, or by a life of penance, or by loss of life itself. Who is there that would not do, or suffer, or sacrifice anything, or even die, if by dying he could make sure of an eternal pardon? Nevertheless it is for none of these conditions that our Divine Lord bestows His forgiveness on us. We could not purchase it, therefore He purchased it for us.

We were "sold gratis," that is, betrayed and lost by sin, and we are "redeemed without money," that is, as we had not wherewith to pay He let us go and forgave us the debt, and yet not till He had paid it Himself. According to the way of wisdom and love, ordained by the Father, the Son of God was incarnate, that He might take a human life, and that having taken it He might have somewhat to lay down for us. "No man taketh it away from me: I have power to lay it down and I have power to take it up again." By the passion of His whole mortal life, and above all, by the last act of shedding for us His Most Precious Blood, Jesus purchased for us the absolution of Baptism and of Penance. It cost Him dear to institute those holy Sacraments. It cost us nothing, for He has freely given them to us. They are ours because they are His, and they are His because He purchased them by the last drop of His divine blood. By an act of sovereign largesse He bestows them upon us. Every several absolution is a Royal pardon, freely and abundantly bestowed, not only " without money and without any price," but notwithstanding our great unworthiness.

And even more than this. That we may be forgiven He requires of us at least a penitent heart; and yet this penitent heart is also His gift. It is by His own preventing grace that we are disposed for the Sacrament of Penance. It is He who awakens supernatural fear by the light of Faith in the reason. It is He who stings the conscience with " the spirit of burning" and the consciousness of past sin. It is He who awakens the hopes of our Heavenly Father's pardon, and gives to the will the impulse which moves it to the Confessional. "No man cometh to the Father but by me," and "no man can come to me except the Father who hath sent me draw him." The Sacrament of Penance then is the Sacrament of the Sovereign Grace of Jesus, and the especial channel and witness of His compassion, and round about the tribunal where He sits in His royal clemency the attraction of his secret inspiration is always moving to and fro to win souls to come to Him. Such is the freeness with which He bestows on men the dear-bought pardon of His Most Precious Blood.

3. Once more the compassion of Jesus shows itself in the Sacrament of Penance by the inexhaustible frequency with which He bestows

upon us absolution after absolution. The angels sinned once and fell. They had no Redemption, no Redeemer; once fallen, fallen to all eternity. Adam sinned once, and fell from life and sonship. He had then no Sacrament of Penance, no Baptism of regeneration. But when sin entered Redemption came with it. And grace brought in a dispensation of forgiveness: first came the virtue of penance as the condition of pardon. Now it is embodied in a Sacrament. "Not as it was by one sin, so also is the gift. For judgment indeed was by one unto condemnation, but grace is of many offences unto justification. For if by one man's offence death reigned through one, much more they who receive abundance of grace out of the gift, and of justice, shall reign in life through one Jesus Christ." Adam's one sin brought death even on those who had not sinned. The Precious Blood of Jesus has brought absolution upon all men, and for all sins countless as the stars of Heaven. There is but one Baptism, but there are many absolutions, for the Sacrament of Penance is a fountain ever-flowing, perennial, and inexhaustible. The silver trumpets proclaimed the jubilee once only in every fifty years, but the Precious Blood cries to us in the Sacrament of Penance at all hours, by day and by night. The pool of Bethsaida in Jerusalem had no healing virtue save only after its waters had been stirred by the visit of an Angel, and then they healed but one sick man: the first alone who could go down into them. Its porches were filled with sufferers languishing with sickness and hope deferred. Again and again for years the gift had been snatched from them even at the moment of arriving; while they were even going down into the waters, another less maimed, and less in need than they were, went down into the waters before them and carried away the grace. To try their faith and patience God hardly opened His hand, and let His power fall only by single drops upon the surface of the pool. Wonderful illustration and contrast. The fountain opened in the heavenly Jerusalem for the sin of man is open day and night; always full of power and grace. Jesus Himself is there the Lord of all Power. Healing and virtue go out from Him with a divine and inexhaustible fulness. It is not the first, or one alone that is healed, but all comers and all sufferers from all lands and at all hours, and no man takes away another's absolution, nor does any one need another's hand to help him to go down into the pool of the Most Precious Blood. God the Holy Ghost is there drawing, sustaining, upholding the weak and maimed, as they go down and are healed one by one. And that not once only, but seventy times seven; as often as men fall, so often they may return, and the same Precious Blood cleanses and heals always as for the first time, with a divine and perfect absolution. Jesus makes no distinction. All who come with the necessary dispositions of heart are healed. For all sins whatsoever, sins after repentance, sins after absolution, sins after a long life of devotion, sins in the full sunshine of His love, there is but one condition – sorrow and the will to sin no more, and where this is, absolution is sure and full.

4. And here again His compassion is almost more luminously shown, that is, in the facility of that which He requires of us as a condition to His absolute pardon. It is in His sovereign gift, and yet not without condition. But this condition He has reduced to the least He could require. Saint Augustine says, "God created us without our co-operation, but He will not justify us without it." In our creation we were passive and unconscious, in our justification we must be

conscious and active. If it were not so, we should not be moral agents, nor would our salvation be by moral means. Though, as I have said, He might have exacted the most that man can do as a condition of eternal life, He requires the least which His moral law exacts. In Baptism He pours out upon us all His gifts of regeneration, sonship, justification, sanctifying grace, and charity, while we are as yet unconscious. Compared with this, indeed, the Sacrament of Penance is more exacting, and it was therefore called by the Holy Fathers "Baptismus laboriosus," a toilsome Baptism, and "post naufragium tabula," a plank after shipwreck, to show that it was the last hope to the lost. Nevertheless, in itself it is a miracle of the facility of Jesus in forgiving sinners.

And first, all that He demands of us is to come to the Sacrament of Penance. He sits all day long in the Confessional, saying, "Come to me all you that labour and are burdened, and I will refresh you." He upbraids us for our unwillingness, "You will not come to me that you may have life." "All the day long have I spread my hands to a people that believeth not and contradicteth me." He pleads with us as if we did Him wrong in destroying ourselves. "Oh, my people, what have I done to thee, or in what have I molested thee, answer thou me?" "Then come and accuse me," saith the Lord. "If your sins be as scarlet they shall be made white as snow, if they be red as crimson they shall be white as wool." Less than this He could not require. At least we must come to Him in the Sacrament of His compassion, that our sins may be forgiven. But I have already shown that even the disposition and the desire to come to Him spring from the inspiration of His own preventing grace, by which He is at all days and all hours drawing souls to Himself. He requires then that we should come to Him, and that we should bring with us at least a sorrow for our sins. It would be a great insincerity and an immoral act to come to Him without sorrow for having offended against Him. This, at least, we owe to Him. If we can do no more, we can at least be sorry. And yet in sorrow there are many degrees so marked, that I might almost say there are many kinds, reaching from the sorrow of fear to the sorrow of love, from the sorrow which springs from a fear of judgment to come to the sorrow which flows from the love of the Sacred

Heart of Jesus. He might justly require of us the sorrow of love, but He requires of us only the sorrow of holy fear, that is from any supernatural motive of faith, such as of the judgment to come, and of eternal death, with a desire of being reconciled to Him. And yet this sorrow is not the sorrow of emotion and tears, but the sorrow of the reason and the will, that is a displeasure against our sins and against ourselves, with a will to sin no more. Unless we have this we should be unfit for absolution, for a will to sin is sin. A will not to sin is the least amends we can make, and this is no more than the retracting of the disobedient will whereby we have offended, and a returning to our obedience as children of God. Together with this sorrow He requires also a truthful and humble confession, a sincere self-accusation in the tribunal of penance, detailing at least the sins we remember, their kind, their number. To this must be joined a resolution to sin no more. Such is the state of heart He requires of us. With this even the greatest of sinners, with all the leprosy of his sin upon him, may come to the Sacrament of Penance, and be cleansed every whit. The prodigal son, after all his wantonness and all his wanderings, with all

his ingratitude, and with the multitude of his
sins upon him, beggared and barefoot, may return to his Heavenly Father with no more than
a "Father, I have sinned against Heaven," and he
is at once forgiven. This is the true facility of the
pardon of Jesus Christ, not the false and delusive
heresy of justification by faith alone, which the
innovators of these later ages have invented, but
the full, free, and sovereign pardon, with which
every penitent soul is received and justified in the
Sacrament of the Compassion of Jesus Christ.

5. There is still one more token of His compassion in this Sacrament of Pardon, and it is the
fervent desire with which He desires to absolve
us of our sins. He loves every several soul with
all the love of His Sacred Heart, and His whole
heart is bent at every moment on the salvation
of those that are lost. He has told us that even
the ninety and nine just are less present to His
loving anxiety, to speak as He has taught us in
the parable of the lost sheep, than the one sinner
doing penance. He seeks out such a soul by His
preventing grace. He surrounds, encompasses,
envelopes it with lights, inspirations, impulses,
attractions of His love and power. Even when
we are unwilling to come to Him, He is yearn-

ing to draw us to Himself. We are distant, and He presses after us, we are unwilling, and He is urgent by His grace. We are cold, and He is on fire with the love of souls. We are tardy in listening, and tardier in coming to Him, and He is ardent and importunate in the reiteration of His calls and inspirations. For He desires to forgive us more than we desire to be forgiven. He loves us even more than we love ourselves. He thirsts for our salvation more than we desire to be saved; and it is in and through and by the Sacrament of Penance that He unfolds to us the full tenderness and compassion of His Sacred Heart in the midst of our miseries and our sins.

Such then are some of the reasons why this Sacrament ought to be an object of our love. It is because Jesus is with us as He was with Magdalen when she stood behind Him weeping, and with Peter after he had denied Him thrice. In it He again receives us to His grace and love, and through it He guides, sustains and consoles the penitent, the fearful, and the tempted. It is the Sacrament of the Presence and the love of the Good Shepherd, and by it all that is expressed in that title of tenderness and compassion is fulfilled to us. "I am come that they may have life, and may have it more abundantly," that is, with all fulness and freeness and facility, again and again as often as they need, and with all the fervour and generosity of the Sacred Heart.

And now this Sacrament of His love to many is necessary, and to all is a fountain of grace.

To those who after Baptism have fallen into mortal sin, it is of necessity. No other Sacrament of life remains to them. No other means of rising from the death of sin to the life of justice is ordained. They cannot raise themselves to life again. The charity of God has departed from them, and the Holy Ghost has withdrawn His habitual grace. The interior acts of then* souls are dead. Their good actions have no power of merit. One act of mortal sin has destroyed all. One such sin in youth has cankered the root of a long life, or one such sin at the close of many years has withered all the growth and fruit of the longest obedience. If they so die, they are lost, and lost for ever. To die out of the love of God is eternal death. How shall they be revived again, except only by this second Sacrament of the dead? If they come with the sorrow of faith and hope, even though they have not charity, the compassion of Jesus will give them a full forgiveness, and breathe into them the breath of life once more.

And lastly to all, even to the holiest, the Sacrament of Penance is a fountain of grace. For it is hard to know ourselves, and it perfects us in self-knowledge; it is hard to be generous in our sorrow, and it perfects our contrition; it is hard to be fervent, and it gives us the spirit of mortification and courage. It is hard to be steadfast and persevering, and it sustains and keeps us up as by the power of the ever-lasting arms. But of this I shall have to speak hereafter. They who habitually frequent this holy Sacrament live in a sweet bondage of love, which is perfect freedom, with a will elevate4 and confirmed in the liberty of the children of God. They who spurn and neglect it, seek for liberty, and fall into a bondage which is heavy and bitter. The sins of the heart, and the sins of the tongue, the temptations of the devil, the yoke of the world, scruples and stings of conscience, fear of death and terrors of judgment to come, these are the wages of those who refuse the light burden and the sweet yoke of Jesus in this Sacrament of His Compassion.

# CHAPTER TWO

# A Means of Self-Knowledge

I have hitherto shown that the Sacrament of Penance is the special manifestation of the compassion of Jesus. As the Church is the manifestation of His Truth to every age, so Penance is the manifestation of His tenderness. Saint Cyprian calls the Church "Sacramentum unitatis ... et Veritatis," u The Sacrament of Unity and Truth;" because by the supernatural Unity of the Church the Truth is incorporated, perpetuated, and promulgated to the world. So Saint Optatus says, "Claves non habent haeretici quas solus Petrus accepit," "The heretics have not the keys, which Peter alone received;" and Saint Augustine, "Unitas tenet unitas dimittit," "Unity binds, unity looses," that is, in the unity of the Church alone the power of loosing from sin is found. Because the Sacrament of Penance is the only revealed channel of the pardon of Jesus Christ to those who fall from baptismal grace. Our Lord, in warning the Church of Laodicea, said, "Because thou sayest I am rich and made wealthy, and have need of nothing; and knowest not, that thou art wretched, and miserable, and poor, and blind, and naked." They were lukewarm and therefore they were self-deceived, and because they were self-deceived they were self-trusting. They believed themselves to be possessed of light and faith, and grace, and know- ledge of themselves, and they knew not their poverty and blindness. Our Lord invites and warns them to come to Him for gold and white raiment, and eye-salve, that is, for sanctifying grace and justification and knowledge of themselves. And this He bestows upon those who are fallen from their baptismal innocence in the Sacrament of Penance.

My present purpose then is to show how the Sacrament of Penance is the means of self-knowledge.

1. And first, because it requires and sustains the habit of self-examination. Once a year, at least, every soul must examine its state before God under pain of sin. Frequent confession re-

quires frequent self-examination. Daily self-examination is the daily preparation for confession, which is the fruit and result of daily self-examination. In this way we are bound by a strong and constraining obligation to a duty which is necessary to salvation, but both unpleasant and difficult. It is absolutely necessary, by the necessity of a means without which there can be no salvation, for without repentance salvation is impossible, and without self-knowledge repentance is impossible. There can be no sorrow or detestation of sins which we know not, nor of acts which we do not know to be sins. And yet, this is an ignorance which will not excuse us. It is vincible, and therefore culpable. Again, if we forget our sins God does not forget them. The sins of childhood and youth and of long years past we may remember no more, but they are written in the book of God's remembrance. All our whole life, so tangled and confused, illegible and dark to our eyes, is all clear and distinct to His. It is a dangerous thing to forget our past. We cannot cast it off except by Penance. Though we forget it we can never escape from its presence. It follows as a shadow, noiseless but inseparable. "Some men's sins are manifest, going

before to judgment; and some men they follow
after." There is but one way to be loosed from
them, and that by the power of the keys. To this,
confession is necessary, and confession without
self-knowledge is impossible.

But self-examination is not only of vital necessity, it is also a painful and displeasing task.
There are two things which we shrink from seeing as they are, God and ourselves. The Sanctity
of God overwhelms and terrifies us. The sight
of our own sins and miseries galls and humbles
us. We have not the courage or the will to look
steadily on either of these things. If we catch
a momentary sight of them we turn away, and
try to lose ourselves in the distractions of other
thoughts. As Saint James says, "If a man be a
hearer of the word, and not a doer: he shall be
compared to a man beholding his own countenance in a glass. For he beheld himself and went
his way, and presently forgot what manner of
man he was."

It wounds our self-love to see our faults, the
sins of commission, the breaches of the ten
commandments, the sins of omission, the ne-
glects, the ingratitude, the meanness of which
we have been guilty. It requires a great sincer-

ity and no little humility to look thoroughly and patiently into ourselves, and to learn the worst of our hearts. It disturbs our peace and breaks our self-complacency. For this reason, multitudes make their self-examination hastily, timidly, and superficially.

But not only is self-examination displeasing; it is also very difficult. For next after God nothing is more inscrutable than the heart which is made in His own likeness. It is a mystery to itself. It conceals itself from our sight, and its motions become unconscious like the circulation of the blood. It is within us, and it is therefore invisible. It is insensible because it is habitual. It is a perpetual motion so rapid that it seems like rest. The thoughts of the intelligence are as countless as the stars of the firmament, the emotions of the heart are as multitudinous as the waves of the sea. The volitions of the will are as inconstant and as continual as the changes and shifts of the wind. "The heart is perverse above all things." It is a deceiver, a flatterer, a dreamer, and a companion of the Tempter. The heart is a deceiver because it is ever changing. It puts on a new colour with its outward circumstances, with its inward trials, with the society in which it may be. It interweaves its motives and misnames its actions. The fiery persuade themselves that they are zealous, the censorious that they are zealous for truth and justice, the slothful and lax that they are benign. It foreshortens its ends so that the ambitious believe themselves to be disinterested, and the worldly to be single-eyed, till they know not for what end they are acting, and while they believe themselves to have only one aim in sight, they have another below .the horizon. But more than this, the heart is a flatterer. It exaggerates all that it has of good: such as its prayers, crosses, alms, devotions, graces, much more its intentions. It excuses all evil. It throws the blame of its faults upon temptations, upon persons, upon circumstances, upon everything but upon itself. It gilds even its sins by soft names and high professions of good intentions and services rendered to God.

The heart is also a dreamer, for it paints itself by the imagination, and pictures itself to itself as a penitent in sackcloth, or a saint in ecstasies. It reads the lives of saints, and dreams itself in their place. It melts also into tears and is moved to passionate emotions before a crucifix or the Blessed Sacrament, like as others shed tears over a tale of imaginary wrongs or of majestic beauty. It puts impulses for volitions, desires for intentions, and intentions for deeds. And, last of all, it is the familiar and playfellow of the Tempter. It listens to him and parleys with him as Achan in Jericho. It courts him as Balaam, and it houses him as Judas did. Of such is the heart capable, and every heart has the whole capacity of all this self-deceit. We have need of a firm eye and an unsparing hand to search it out, and unless we be sustained and even bound to this painful task, few have severity enough with themselves to do it as they ought. It is the Sacrament of Penance, then, which binds us to this duty, and the oftener we come to it the oftener we are compelled to search out the secret working of our hearts and to know them with a true knowledge.

2. Again, it places us in the light of the Cross. The reason why we all see our sinfulness so little is because we so little appreciate the Sanctity of God. Our lives seen in the light of the world, or of our own self-love, or of our flattering friends, are very different from the same life, seen in the light of the presence of God. Thomas a Kempis says, "Sordet in conspectu judicis, quod fulget in conspectu opeantis," "What looks bright

in the eyes of the doer looks base in the sight
of the Judge." When Isaias saw the Lord upon
His throne his first consciousness was that he
was a man of unclean lips Daniel fell at the feet
of the angel of the Lord, and his beauty was
turned into corruption. Saint John, when in vision he saw the Lord, on whose bosom he had
lain, fell at His feet as dead. It was the light of
the Divine Presence which revealed the sin and
the infirmity of even such Saints as these. Such
in its measure is the effect of the Sacrament of
Penance upon us. We kneel under the light of
the Ever-Blessed Trinity, and of the Incarnate
Word, and of His holy Passion, and of the Divine Soul of Jesus, which in its agony expiat-
ed our imperfect contrition, and of the Sacred
Heart which gives out its illumination by the
wound in the side of Jesus. All these lights come
down upon us as we kneel in the confessional,
and in them we see not only ourselves, our past
life, our present character, but the law of God
which we have broken, its letter and its spirit,
what it forbids, what it enjoins upon our obedience, our fidelity, and our generosity. And by
this clearer knowledge of the rule we can detect our deviations from its rectitude. We never

see ourselves more clearly than when we kneel
under the crucifix in the Sacrament of Penance,
and the oftener we kneel there the clearer grows
the light of the knowledge of self in the presence
of God and at the feet of Jesus Christ.

3. And further, one great hindrance to
self-knowledge is the spirit of self-defence. The
Pharisee, who stood and prayed by himself,
thanking God that he was not as other men are,
is the type of those who turn from the Confessional. The Publican is the type of the Penitent
upon his knees. For what is the Sacrament of
Penance, but the Sacrament of self-accusation.
We are all tempted to excuse ourselves. When
the eyes and ears of the world are open upon us,
we are all full of apologies, or denials. It needs
the heroic humility of a Saint to suffer and be
silent; like Saint Vincent de Paul, who, when
falsely accused in the anti-chamber of the King
of France, went down on his knees and took the
shame without a word.

But in the Confessional we can make no excuses. We know that all is known to Him who
sits there unseen: "For the word of God is living and effectual, and more piercing than any
two-edged sword; and reaching unto the divi-

sion of the soul and the spirit, of the joints also, and the marrow, and is a discerner of the thoughts and intents of the heart. Neither is there any creature invisible in His sight: but all things are naked and open to His eyes, to whom our speech is." We know that we can suppress nothing; that He saw all, and heard all, and knows all before we speak, and that He puts our truth on trial, in requiring us to tell out our whole tale against ourselves. We cannot give a turn even to an expression, or pass over a single point, for He knows all things. Not a jot or a tittle may be changed, for the Divine scrutiny searches the heart at the time of the confession as well as at the time of the sin.

4. And besides this, the Sacrament of Penance gives us the guidance of another. We know well that no man can trust himself to be judge in his own case. With all our profession of sincerity we are warped when we are judging of ourselves. We are unconscious of our words and acts. We note instantly in another the very things of which we are not aware in ourselves. Nay, we detect the least impetuosity in others, and fail to see the most headstrong passion in ourselves. As our Divine Lord has said: "we can see the mote in

our brother's eye, and cannot perceive the beam which is in our own;" and therefore He has ordained the Sacrament of Penance, in which, go when we may, we find at least one man in the world who is a true friend to us – at least one friend who will not flatter us.

And more, the Priest in the Confessional is not only an impartial judge, but also a practised one. Like as a physician, who by long use knows all the symptoms of disease, who can tell its premonitory signs> the manifestations of its presence, and the effects which it leaves behind it: so is the Priest, who is divinely ordained to sit and judge "between leprosy and leprosy," and to discern whether it be only rising, or in full power, or departing. A physician will often discover disease where no one suspects it, and by signs which to others are unperceived. Not only the beat of the pulse and the colour of the skin, but its texture, the light of the eye, the harshness of the hair, and other such tokens, give evidence of the presence of disease. In like manner, in the Confessional, long habit of dealing with the pathology of souls enables a Confessor at once to discover symptoms which the Penitent does not know or even imagine.

But further, he is not only practised, and his perceptions quickened by experience and use, but he is also enlightened to discover even that which the Penitent may not say, or know. There is a special light vouchsafed to those who guide souls. They are moved often to say more than they are aware of, and to waken up whole periods of memory and trains of thought, which the Penitent has either forgotten, or failed to perceive. Sometimes a question suggests a new and truer estimate of actions which have been altogether misunderstood. Sometimes it seems like an intuition, or a gift of supernatural insight, as indeed it is. Sometimes perhaps consciously, often unconsciously like men that work in mines, before they are aware, they strike through into open day, and find themselves all of a sudden in the light of the sun. The Holy Spirit makes use of the Confessor to illuminate the Penitent, either by enlightening him directly, or by using him to reflect a light which he hardly sees himself.

In these ways, then, they who frequent the Sacrament of Penance are ever advancing in a truer knowledge of themselves.

5. And lastly, there is another light vouchsafed to them directly, an illumination which falls inwardly upon the conscience from the increase of spiritual grace. For, as every Sacrament conveys an increase of grace, and every grace brings light, so every time we worthily receive the Sacrament of Penance we receive a greater inward light. Self-examination prepares for the Sacrament, and the Sacrament elevates it to a supernatural knowledge of self. At the beginning we see ourselves but dimly, and can discern little with truth. We "see men, as it were trees, walking;" but in a little while all becomes self-evident as the light of day. It was by this internal light that Saints have called themselves the "chief of sinners;" that Saint Clare wondered that her sisters did not shun her as "one stricken with the plague." Saint Vincent Ferrer used to say, that he daily grew worse and worse. It was this that made Saint Francis Borgia construct what he called the ladder of confusion. That is, he first placed himself before the Holy Trinity, and was overwhelmed by the contrast of the uncreated Sanctity and our created infirmity. Next he placed himself in the light of the Sacred Humanity, and confounded himself at the sight of

his own nature, so shattered and defaced; then in the presence of the Immaculate Mother of God, a mere creature, though God's mother, and humbled himself for the soils and stains of both original and actual sin; then before the Holy Angels, and condemned his own tardy and lingering obedience by the energy and fervour of their ministries; then of the Saints, and by their perseverance he measured his own inconstancy; then of the servants of God on earth, of whom he professed himself to be the least; then of the souls in Purgatory, of whom the least humble is more profoundly humble than any Saint on earth; then of the souls that are lost, confessing that if they had received his grace they would have been holier and more penitent than himself.

Such was his practice for some two hours a day, during which he examined himself by the ten commandments, and after each made acts of contrition for his many and grievous transgressions. Such was the self-examination of a Saint. He had no difficulty in finding matter of humiliation, though he had so little; we find it a hard task, though we have sinned so much. And why? It is because our internal perceptions

of God and of His Kingdom are faint and dim.
The knowledge of God and of ourselves comes
and goes, and varies together. Saint Francis, who
on Mount Alvernia received from the flaming
Seraph on the Cross the five piercing rays which
imprinted on him the stigmata of Jesus, spent
the whole of a lonely night under the alternate
illumination of this knowledge of God and of
himself, pouring out his soul in repeating: " Oh,
my God! how great art Thou; how little am I."
From whence, then, did all these great Saints receive this profound light of self-knowledge, but
from the life of Penance, of which this Sacrament is the source and perfection.

From all that has been said two plain practi-
cal truths are evident. First, that we may never
think that we know all we might of ourselves.
In the heart there are so many windings and
doubles, so many masks and disguises, so many
false lights, so much paint upon the face, and
so many artificial expressions of countenance,
that it is certain we deceive ourselves as well
as others. They who know themselves best are
only least deceived. This we may understand by
thinking how different our past life looks now.
At the time we thought it all fair, just as we think

our present life. We suspected nothing wrong in things which now seem manifestly wrong. We were as confident of our motives and intentions then as we are now. But a few years have thrown a new light upon it all. A few years hence and we shall see our present as now we see our past. How different all will look upon a deathbed. Then a new and true light will reveal a multitude of secrets, and show much that we never believed possible How different all will appear when we look back upon our earthly life from the world beyond the grave, in the hour of the particular judgment, and at the moment of entering Purgatory, and at the general judgment of the last day. Then all masks shall be taken off from all faces, and we shall know as we are known and see as we are seen. Then many who have seemed to know each other, parents, children, friends, pastors, penitents, shall know each other for the first time, and wonder at the vain show in which they lived and died. We must, therefore, be always pressing onwards in the knowledge of self, with much self-mistrust and with a sincere desire to know the worst of ourselves.

And next, we may learn never to fear when we see the worst of ourselves. To see more sins is no sign of committing more, but of greater knowledge of self. And if we have more knowledge then more light, and if more light then more of the presence of the Holy Ghost. For when He comes into the heart He casts a broad light upon it, but conceals Himself. We see ourselves, not Him, and He reveals to us, not the things which are pleasant to us, but those that are displeasing to Himself; not our graces, or prayers, or good dispositions, but our sins and omissions, our inward faults, our unstable wills, our unloving hearts. He reveals to us that we are poor and miserable, outcast, blind, and naked, that we may buy of Him gold tried in the fire, and white raiment, and eye-salve to open our eyes, that we may see ourselves as we appear now in His sight and in the light of His eternal throne.

# Chapter Three

# Perfecting Our Contrition

We have seen how the Sacrament of Penance requires, and infuses, and perfects the knowledge of ourselves, and next I wish to show how in like manner it requires, and infuses, and perfects our contrition. It is not only true that they who are least contrite go less often to confession, but also that they who go often become most contrite, and that their contrition is elevated and matured by frequenting the Sacrament of Penance.

Now it is hardly necessary to state here in words that contrition is of two kinds, the contrition of fear and the contrition of love. But in the production of this sorrow there are many distinct motives, progressive in their operation, and ascending in their kind from the lowest sorrow which is necessary to the Sacrament to the highest, which is a special gift of God.

1. And first, there is a sorrow which springs from the knowledge of our sins. This is the first and lowest motive of contrition, the deadliness and baseness of our sins seen in the light of the presence of God.

But at the outset of our conversion, or life of penance, our sins, though they be so many, all seem as one. They are all mingled in confusion, and they conceal each other and themselves by their multitude and their complication. A mountain of sand and a heap of stones seem to us at first to be but one object. It is only as we draw near to them, and begin to look into them, and to separate the grains and the stones, that we begin to find their number. Moreover, so long as the effects of a sinful, or of a worldly life are upon the heart, it is stunned and dim-sighted. It is only gradually that we begin to see the innumerable multitude of our sins, and then they seem to us to surpass all number. As we draw near to them, they disengage themselves and stand out one by one, and what we once thought from a distance to be but one, separates itself into an infinity of particles. So our sins stand out, each one in its distinctness of kind, of number, and of circumstance.

And as this process is advancing, so also our sorrow is increasing. We had in the beginning a sorrow for the sin of our life, seen in the tangle and confusion of our first conversion. But now we feel a sorrow for each as we remember them one by one; and a greater sorrow it may be for each, one by one, than before we felt for all together. I have already attempted to describe this process of growing illumination, by which we gradually attain a more adequate perception of our state before God. I say a more adequate, because, after all, it is but a small part of the great and complex multitude of the sins of our life, which we ever see in this world. They were all present one by one, in their distinctness and in their guilt, before the Divine vision of Jesus, in the garden of His agony: they are all written in the Book of His remembrance: they will all be revived before our eyes in the particular judgment, but now our fullest perception of them is inadequate, and falls far short of these true and Divine revelations of what we are. Still as they come out more and more into the light, so they become each one a subject of sorrow. Though our Lord does not require of us a separate act of sorrow for each separate sin, yet each separate sin as it comes to mind will be a new motive to sorrow, and though the act of sorrow be but one, the motives will be many. But all this may be no more than the sorrow of holy fear, awakened by the deadliness and the baseness of our sins, as they stand out before the conscience illuminated by the Spirit of God.

2. There is then another kind of sorrow, more pure and generous, which springs from a sense of the love of God.

He loved us while we were yet in sin. The Prodigal in the far country remembered his Father, and his Father's love. The consciousness that his Father loved him still, moved him to return, and to accuse himself with a profound humility. The sense of his unworthiness, and of his ingratitude, was sharpened by the sense of his Father's tenderness. The sunshine of his childhood, and of his boyhood, and the light of his Father's countenance, rose full upon him once more, and he knew that although he was all changed, his Father was still the same; that though his heart was hardened, his Father's heart was yet full of loving kindness. All this he felt while he was still far off in his misery. How much more when his Father fell upon his neck, gave him the kiss of peace, and arrayed him once more in the raiment and the ring of sonship. Then the consciousness of his own selfishness and ingratitude deepened all his contrition. It was keen while he was yet trembling in his sins, but keener far when his sins had been forgiven.

The absolution of his Father's love elevated him to a higher, and to a more generous, because a more loving sorrow. So it is in the Sacrament of Penance, when we have indeed " tasted that the Lord is sweet," and have been made the subjects of His miraculous love. When we have received from Him the pledge that "when as yet we were sinners, Christ died for us," and while we were yet in our sins, our Heavenly Father loved us with an everlasting love, then we begin to understand the words of the Holy Ghost, "God so loved the world as to give His only begotten Son, that whosoever believeth in Him may not perish, but have life everlasting." "In this is charity: not as though we had loved God, but because He hath first loved us, and sent His Son to be a propitiation for our sins." Then we see that but for this changeless love we should long since have died eternally; that by it He bore with us in childhood, in the times of our ignorance; in youth, in the time of our sin; and in manhood, in the time of our cool and deliberate self-love. It is "the mercies of the Lord that we are not consumed; because His tender mercies have not failed." We wake up to know that we have been encompassed and enveloped in the love of God, that we have been borne up and sustained by it, even when we thought nothing of Him, nay, even when we were provoking Him every day, as if the prodigal after his return had begun to carry himself loftily, and to forget his past unworthiness, and even to relapse, and after his relapse to be once more forgiven.

For such is our state. Again and again we have sinned like the Prodigal, and again and again our Heavenly Father has received us, as He did at the first time with the kiss of peace and a perfect absolution. It was this thought that made Saint Catherine of Genoa so profoundly contrite. In the progress of her repentance, a ray of God's love so intensely burning and piercing was infused into her soul, that all appeared to her in a new light, her past and her present life, her sins of thought, word, and deed, her sins of commission and omission, all bore a new meaning, and received a new interpretation.

3. Again, there is another motive of sorrow, that is, the special sense of our personal sinfulness. I have already spoken of the sorrow arising from the knowledge of our sins, but this sorrow for our personal sinfulness is different in kind. Many who are covered with a multitude of sins have little of it. Some have most of it, whose sins are lightest and fewest, for it is a perception depending upon what we are. And the most saintly hearts are the most illuminated. I have already quoted Saint Clare, Saint Vincent Ferrer, and Saint Francis Borgia as proofs. I might take one more example, and that from Saint Paul, who says, "that Christ Jesus came into this world to save sinners, of whom I am the chief; and this he said not by way of a pious exaggeration, but because of the knowledge he had of himself. It is no rash and rhetorical overstatement, but the true expression of his inward consciousness, as the following reasons will show: First of all, we do not know so much *formal* evil of any one as we know of ourselves. We may, indeed, know more material evil of many, that is, we may know of many who have fallen into sins more glar-

ing and scandalous, from which we have been preserved. But the formal evil of actions is to be estimated by the internal acts, and these by the light we possess, and by the operations of the Holy Spirit, against whom we have sinned. It is certain, therefore, that lesser sins against greater light are more formally sinful, than greater sins against lesser light. And it is this we may know of ourselves, but we cannot know of any other. Our Lord one day said to Saint Mechtild-is: "Come and see the least in the kingdom of Heaven, and thou shalt know the fountain of loving kindness. And she saw a man clothed in a green garment, with smooth hair, of middle stature, and very beautiful countenance. She asked, Who art thou? and he said, I was upon earth a robber, and a malefactor, and never did I any thing good. She asked, How didst thou enter into this joy? He answered, All the evils I did were done not out of wickedness, but as by custom, and because I knew no better, because I was reared up in them by my parents, wherefore by penance I found mercy with God."

Again, we do not know of any one, who has received so great graces as we have. Others may have received more, but we do not know it. We

are able to measure in some degree, but that
most imperfectly, the numberless gifts which
God has bestowed upon each one of us; that
is, in our Baptism, Confirmation, Commu-
nions, and Penance, in our childhood, youth,
and manhood, the lights, inspirations, stings of
conscience, and impulses of heart, which have
perpetually moved and sustained us. All this
inner world of our own God knows, and so
does each one for himself. But of another no
man can judge. Even the nearest do not know
how much grace God has bestowed upon others. How much less can we know and judge
those who are afar off. We are conscious not
only of the abundance of Sacramental graces,
but of the graces out of the Sacraments, which
have filled the atmosphere in which we breathe,
and pervade every moment of our lives. So far
as we know, none have ever received so many,
none have ever been so followed and sustained,
so invited and solicited, so warned and so en-
couraged. All the wonderful long-suffering and
patience, the delicacy and generosity of the Holy
Spirit with us from our Baptism, we know. It
is like the continuous beat of our heart, which
we have felt from our earliest childhood. We

are personally conscious of our own spiritual life, but we can only know that of another by hearsay, and a most imperfect and fragmentary observation. And as we know of no one who has received so many graces as we have, so we know of no one who has so little corresponded with them.

Out of many lights we have followed few, and out of many invitations we have accepted only a scanty number. Many graces we have altogether lost by resistance, and many with which we ought to have corresponded generously and adequately we have hardly answered at all, or with an ungenerous reserve. What might we not have been now, if we had been true to our Baptismal grace? How soon it was soiled, how wantonly it was squandered; how tardily and reluctantly we answered to the grace of conversion, which led us back to penance; how little time we retained our first absolution, or the fervour of our first communion, or the strength of our confirmation, or the spirit of holy fear which came upon us in our chastisements, or the spirit of praise which sprung up within us* in the days of consolation. All our whole life has been a long series of graces given profusely and little used, of Divine generosity and human illiberality, of inexhaustible mercy on God's part and niggardly returns on ours. It is not only then the sight of our sins, of which I spoke first, but the sight of ourselves, and of our sins, as committed in the midst of such graces, and by one who has been singled out for such endless and countless mercies, that ought to deepen our sorrow with a new motive, and to soften us with a peculiar sense of our own personal sinfulness.

4. But there is still another kind of sorrow less personal, and more generous than the last, and that is, the sorrow which springs from the passion of Jesus, "They shall look upon Me, whom they have pierced: and they shall mourn for Him." With the marvellous precision of thought, which marks the Theology of the Church, a distinction is made between the imperfect and the perfect contrition, that is between attrition and contrition, properly so called. The word attrition signifies the bruising of the heart, as by a fall, or by a blow, but contrition signifies the bruising to powder, the perfect breaking up of the hardness of the heart. The former expresses well the action of grace, but the latter the action, which love alone can

accomplish, and such is the distinction I have tried to mark between a sorrow for our sins and a sorrow for our personal sinfulness.

There is, however, another word in common use, still more expressive, and with a distinction more clearly and finely marked, and that is, compunction. This signifies a piercing, and a piercing together with our Lord Jesus Christ, a partaking in His wounds, as compassion is partaking in His sufferings. As contrition then is the perfection of attrition, compunction is the perfection of contrition. It is its mature and ultimate form, and stands to the previous kinds of sorrow as the Beatitudes to the gifts and graces of the Holy Ghost. After the sorrow and shame, which spring from contemplating the guilt, and baseness, and deadliness of sin, comes the sorrow which springs from God's love and our own ingratitude, and then from the sufferings of the Sacred Heart in Gethsemani, and on Calvary, and from our personal guilt towards Him who loved us so much, and has been loved by us so little.

The motives of this sorrow are specially, the Bloody Sweat, the five Sacred Wounds, the wounds of the Sacred Countenance, and the

Divine Sorrow of the Sacred Heart. "All the day long have I spread forth My hands to a people that believeth not and contradicteth Me." And in His outstretched palms, the print of the nails reproaches us with the sharpness of death, which He overcame for us, and for the hardness of heart with which we have crucified Him again and again unto ourselves. He is always before our eyes set forth crucified among us, and crying to us from the Cross, "O all ye that pass by the way, attend and see if there be any sorrow like to My sorrow: for He hath made a vintage of Me, as the Lord spoke in the day of His fierce anger." Truly we pass by and leave Him to hang all alone upon His Cross for us; we pass by, and pass on to our pleasure, our forgetfulness, our ease, and the remembrance of His ineffable sorrow leaves no impression upon our lives, and casts no shadow over our careless hearts. We go all the day without remembering Him. We look upon the Crucifix, without accusing ourselves of having caused His great sorrow, and of robbing His Cross of its fruit in ourselves, and of renewing His Passion, by returning to the sins for which He died. Now this sorrow, once conceived, is a sorrow which will grow as long as life lasts, for the contemplation of the Passion of Jesus is inexhaustible, and at every new manifestation of His love and of His sufferings, casts a new light upon our sins. And here we have the key to what we have already seen, namely, that the greatest Saints have sorrowed most for sin. They have sorrowed most, because they have known most of His love and Passion, and because they were most like Him, in His hatred for sin, and His zeal for the glory of His Father.

Such then was the illuminated compunction of Saint Paul, when he called himself the chief of sinners. It is the perfection of such sorrow to be self- forgetting. As it is purified of self, it remembers only Jesus. Saint Mary Magdalen, when she hurried to the Pharisee's house, and stood behind our Divine Redeemer, weeping, was full of sorrow and of love; and yet what was her contrition then, compared with her sorrow when she stood by the Cross of Jesus on Calvary, or when she lingered all alone and weeping at the empty Sepulchre, and knew not where they had laid Him.* What made this change in her sorrow, but the Passion of Jesus, the true and Divine Crucifix on which she had gazed on Calvary. We read in the writings of Blessed Angela, of Foligno, that she passed through eighteen degrees of compunction, beginning with a confession in which, through natural shame, she concealed her sins, and ending in the sorrow of the Saints. After she had made many steps in the way of contrition, she tells us that one day, at the sight of the Crucifix, a flood of sorrow and self-accusation came upon her, with a sense of her ingratitude to Him whom her sins had pierced, so that she was overwhelmed with a grief beyond control. And ever afterwards the sight of a Crucifix was enough to throw her into a tumult of sorrow, in so much that her companions were forced to hide it from her. Such is the contrition of a soul pierced with the consciousness of the wounds of Jesus, and wounded itself by them. It says, with Saint Paul, "With Christ I am nailed to the Cross," and with Him it sorrows, and for His sake.

5. Lastly, there is a sorrow which crowns all, and is the special gift of the Holy Ghost, a sorrow which Saint Paul calls "the sorrow that is according to God, working penance steadfast unto salvation." Our Lord promised this sorrow, when He said, "When He," that is the Holy Ghost, "is come, He will convince the world of

sin." We have seen how a penitent who brings nothing but the sorrow of Faith and Hope to the Sacrament of Penance, receives therein the sanctifying grace of the Holy Ghost, and Charity; and by the infusion of Charity is raised once more to the life of God, and elevated to union with Him. Thenceforth he is able to make acts of perfect contrition. Though perhaps at the time of his absolution he may not do so, yet he is thereby placed in a state of habitual power so to do. And all the motives of contrition of which I have spoken, begin to work upon his heart, and his whole disposition of soul towards God becomes more filial, loving, and generous; and the vision of God, and of himself, grows more clear and abiding and his sense of the love and of. the Passion of Jesus more vivid and subduing, so that day by day his sorrow is purified of servile fear and of selfish desires. In the measure in which the sanctification of the soul is deepened and enlarged the sorrow for sin is increased.

That which hinders sorrow for sin is sin itself. The more sin is cast out, the more sorrow enters. Therefore, as we have seen, the greatest Saints have always had the greatest sorrow for their own sins, and also for the sins of others. They have lamented all their life long, with a vehemence of self-accusation, for acts which others, perhaps, would have hardly confessed at all. Saint Teresa speaks of herself in a language which would make us suppose her guilty of great and grave sins, when from her confessors we know that she never committed a mortal sin. The cause of this is the supernatural light in which she estimated sin, as in the light of God Himself. The consciousness that in sinning we have grieved and resisted the Holy Ghost our Sanctifier, our patient Guide, and our Helper, who from our Baptism has never left us for a moment, unless we have forsaken Him, and at the first relenting of our hearts has returned to us, to inhabit our whole soul in all its power of action and affection, is the last perfection of a contrite heart.

We have seen how the sorrows of Saint Mary Magdalen increased in purity and intensity as she drew nearer to the Passion and Cross of Jesus; but there were others with her on Calvary, whose sorrow for sin was deeper and more profound than hers. The Beloved Disciple knew even more profoundly the deadliness of sin, and the Divine hatred against it. In the heart of the

Immaculate Mother of God, seven dolours, like the currents of seven seas, met together. She who was without sin knew best of all creatures the baseness and deadliness of sin, the love of God, the personal sinfulness of men, the passion of her Divine Son for sinners; and because she had no sin, therefore her sorrow was according to God, profound, supernatural, and intense, to the full measure of which a creature is capable.

There was then never any sorrow greater than hers, except one, the sorrow of Jesus himself. His sorrow in Gethsemani is the type of perfect contrition. It was a sorrow for sin, and for the love of God, free, pure, and generous. "Velut mare contritio tua." His contrition was as the sea, profound, overwhelming, and immense: and in proportion as we are conformed to His Sacred Heart, our contrition will be like His great sorrow. The thought of God, of His Glory, of His love, rises over everything else. As Saint Catherine of Genoa says of Purgatory, it is not so much the remembrance of sin, as the love of God, which causes the pain of the holy souls. For their sorrow ascending to God, is like His own sorrow. It is like the Divine displeasure with which the Holy Ghost looks upon our sins, when, as Saint Paul says, we "grieve" Him, it is the grief of God Himself. The sorrow of Jesus is the sorrow also of a human heart, but the grief of the Holy Ghost is altogether and alone Divine.

Such is the universal and efficacious, the supernatural and tranquil sorrow, which the Church calls perfect contrition, raised from motive to motive, and matured by the presence and operations of the Holy Ghost in the soul.

And now, although such a sorrow is the gift of God, yet it is to be sought and to be obtained in and through the Sacrament of Penance. I have already shown to whom it is necessary, and to whom it is beneficial. Some confessions, therefore, are of obligation, and some of devotion. We may leave aside the confessions of necessity and of obligation, for I am now chiefly speaking of confessions of devotion. I desire to show that frequent confession is a great and manifold benefit, even to those to whom it is not necessary. I have shown how it exacts and sustains the habit of a stated reckoning with ourselves, how it renews our absolution and our peace with God, how it infuses a new Sacramental grace every time we receive it, and how it continually elevates and perfects our attrition, changing it into contrition; and our contrition, illuminating it and changing it into compunction. And all these benefits are obtained by those who come worthily to the Sacrament of Penance week by week, even though they bring only venial sins, or even nothing but a renewed accusation and contrition for mortal sins long ago confessed and forgiven.

And in order that frequent confession may be neither a mere habit, nor a too familiar act, we shall do well to keep alive the habit of making acts of contrition not only day by day, but often every day. It is a good and useful practice to make a list of the sins by which we have displeased God, or to which we are most tempted, and to repeat them name by name every morning, together with a list of the graces most opposed to them, and to ask them of the Holy Spirit, with acts of sorrow for the many times we have grieved Him by the faults of which we have been guilty. In this way we may renew our sorrow for the mortal sins already confessed and absolved for the venial sins not yet confessed, and for the entanglement and confusion of thoughts, words, deeds, and omissions which make up our daily life. If we need an act of contrition, we can find none better than the Name of Jesus: as, "Jesus, I am sorry for the baseness and the multitude of my sins. Jesus I am sorry, because of the goodness of Thy Father and my Father, whom I have offended. Make Thou my sorrow to be deeper, more loving and more fervent until the hour of my death."

# CHAPTER FOUR

# The Sacrament of Reparation

We have seen the shame and sorrow of Saint Mary Magdalen, in the house of Simon, the Pharisee, in the beginning of her conversion, and then the courage and fidelity of her devotion at the foot of the Cross; and now when all was over, when she had watched the sufferings of Jesus to. the last, and had helped to lay Him in His tomb, when all her service of love was done, her heart was still busy about His memory. She went and brought spices and ointments, and rested on the Sabbath-day, intending to anoint Him on the morrow. Beautiful and wonderful fidelity of tender and grateful love. Jesus was dead, what could now avail these ministries of devotion to His memory? Yet they were due and sweet. She owed them to Him to whom she owed all; and though He should know nothing of them, they were sweet to her for His sake. In this we see the character of generous contrition.

From the hour that she washed our Saviour's feet with her tears, and wiped them with the hair of her head, she laid aside for ever the vanity and luxury with which she had offended His Divine Sanctity. Thenceforward all her life was a perpetual mortification of her natural self. Saint Peter, after he had wept bitterly for his three denials, entered upon a life of reparation to his Divine Master, which had its proportionate end and crown in his inverted cross on Mount Janiculum. Saint Paul says, that in him first Christ Jesus had shewn forth all patience, forasmuch as he had been "a persecutor and contumelious;" therefore, he spent a long life in reparation, which he describes as "always bearing about in our body the mortification of Jesus." His long life of supernatural toil and suffering was crowned at last by the lictor's sword, at the Salvian Waters, with the diadem of martyrdom. Such was the spirit of reparation among the disciples of Jesus, free, spontaneous, and unsparing even unto death. In this we have a beautiful example of the spirit of satisfaction, which is infused and perfected in the Sacrament of Penance.

Now, the Church teaches us that the only condition to absolution is contrition, including confession either in fact or in desire, so that satisfaction, or the penance which follows after, perfects, but is not of the essence of contrition. Though it be imposed, nevertheless it is willingly accepted, and, therefore, is a free and spontaneous return for a free and spontaneous pardon. And the effect of it is to expiate and to make reparation; to expiate the pains due to us for the sins which have been absolved by a voluntary chastisement of self, and to make reparation to the Sacred Heart of Jesus which we have wounded by our ingratitudes. Such is the penance imposed on us in our absolution. But it also sets before us what ought to be the life-long fruit of this Sacrament. It teaches that all the life of those who have been absolved ought to be spent in satisfaction for the past.

First, I will try to explain what this spirit of reparation consists of, and then will shew how it is infused and perfected in the Sacrament of Penance.

1. It consists then, first, in an indignation against ourselves. Saint Paul, writing to the Corinthians, expresses this as follows: "That you were made sorrowful according to God, how great carefulness it worketh in you: yea defence, yea indignation, yea fear, yea desire, yea zeal, yea revenge." They, indeed, felt this indignation for the shame brought on them by the sins of another. How much more reason for keener indignation have we for the sins which we have each one committed against God; for the sins of deliberation whereby we have grieved and resisted His Holy Spirit, contradicted His will, broken His law, and outraged His love. God made us for Himself – for His love and for His glory. He made us capable of knowing and loving, worshipping and serving, of praising and glorifying Him, but we have robbed and defrauded Him. We have borne bitter fruits or have stood barren before Him. Is it possible to fail of the end of our creation more than we have failed?

Moreover, we have need to be indignant with ourselves for our habitual inclination to self, for the love and worship of our own will, for our waste of life and time, and the natural powers which God has given us: for the neglect of our visitations and opportunities, of graces and of sacraments. If we examine one of our sins of commission, or of omission, in the light of God s presence, and by the love of the Incarnation and Passion of Jesus, or in the light of the Holy Ghost, we shall find abundant matter for indignation against ourselves: if for nothing else, for our instability in good. We seem to have so little affinity to it, and so little union with it, that we vary and waver between good and evil, as if they were alike to us, and indifferent in themselves

Now, any one who has attained such a knowledge of himself, as I endeavoured to explain in the last two chapters, must feel spring up in him shame, and zeal, and indignation against himself, with a desire to humble and punish himself, and to take, as Saint Paul says, a revenge.

2. Next to this comes a sense of gratitude. Blessed Alvarez used to say, that his faults were like so many windows which let in the light of the love of God upon his soul, for each one of them became a fresh evidence of the patience and tenderness of God towards him. How much more the sins of which we have been guilty, and the faults which we carry to confession every

week. The love and compassion of God which, like a great stream, is continually descending upon us every day, would awaken gratitude in a stone. He raised us from spiritual death in Baptism, and has raised us again and again in Penance, sometimes, as Saint Augustine says, like Jairus's daughter, just dead; sometimes like the widow's son, already carried out to burial; sometimes like Lazarus, four days buried in the grave. He has received us back again like the prodigal, not once only but many times. He has re-invested us with our lost inheritance, and, perhaps, called us to a higher path in His kingdom, and given us special illuminations, and special union with Himself. If these things do not elicit gratitude we must be dead indeed. Now, the Sacrament of Penance is the special manifestation of these gifts and graces, and, therefore, the special means of awaking us to a sense of them.

3. A third element in the spirit of reparation, is generosity, And this is luminously manifested to us in the sovereign grace of absolution. In it God gives us pardon with a fulness, a freeness, a facility, and inexhaustible frequency which exceeds all we can ask or think. Even the most

soiled and unworthy He restores to His peace
and love. Our Heavenly Father keeps back nothing from us. All that is communicable He gives
to us. Jesus gives us all that He can part with.
The Holy Ghost gives Himself and all things
again and again, seventy-times-seven, as often as
we turn and repent. Now this ought, at least, to
awake in us some generosity in return. At least
we ought to be as generous in forgiving others
as He is in forgiving us.

If God gives Himself to us, surely we cannot
be slow to give of our substance in alms. If He
should call us to forsake all and to follow His
steps, we could not refuse to rise up and to go
after Him. If He should draw us to give ourselves to Him, as He has given Himself for us,
how could we hang back?

4. Another disposition included in the spirit
of reparation, is a hatred not only of the least
actual sin but also of lukewarmness. Our absolution shews us how great a price was paid for us;
how much it cost Him to institute this Sacrament of His free compassion on our behalf. It is
the fruit of His Agony in the garden and of His
Passion upon the Cross. Nothing could have
obtained it for us but His most Precious Blood.

This sets sin before us as an insult to His Cross – as a wound in the Sacred Heart – as a betrayal of Jesus, sometimes for a piece of money, or for a pleasure with fair professions of fidelity, that is, we also betray Him by a kiss. If He loved us so as to consume Himself for us in the fire of His charity, how without great personal sin can we be lukewarm towards Him? Cold returns for warm friendship are intolerable among men. Neglect will separate those who have never otherwise offended each other. So between us and Jesus. He is all love for us, and we have treated Him as if He had done nothing for our good and suffered nothing in our stead. It is very slowly that we come to perceive this fault in our hearts, but when once perceived, we know and we feel that we can never do enough for Him. All that we do seems feeble and cold.

5. Lastly, the spirit of reparation contains in it a love of the Cross. Jesus loved it for our sakes. If we love Him, we must love it for His sake. We laid it upon Him by our sins, at least we ought to be willing to lay it upon ourselves in reparation. Saint Paul says, "They that are Christ's have crucified their flesh with the vices and concupiscences." First, in Penance and the mortification

of the sin that dwells in us; and next, in the life of reparation which springs from a generous love of our Divine Master.

For this cause, the crosses which come upon us from the hand of God ought to be borne with submission and with sweetness, and the crosses which come from the hand of men ought likewise to be received with patience, and even with gladness. They do but conform us to Jesus in the two great perfections of His humility. To be like Him is necessary to salvation, and it is also sweet to those who love Him. Nay, if we be generous we shall choose to be like Him in His humiliation and in His Cross, rather than to be prosperous and in honour. It is a hard lesson, but a true one. Even if we knew that we might be saved with equal certainty in a life of fair days, and bright lights, and smooth, even ways, a generous love to our Divine Lord would make us choose the shadow of His life and the sharpness of His path, because it unites us more closely to Him if only by imitation and by the evidence of our love and gratitude. If a brother or a friend were in the field of battle, it would be still lawful for us to enjoy the pleasant things of home as when they were with us. But an instinct of generous affection would make us turn from pleasures and find consolation even in privations, as a way of sharing in hardship with those we love, and manifesting our love to them. If this be true of kinsmen and friends in the imperfect state of our humanity, how much more of Him who is not only our Friend and Brother, but also our Saviour and our Redeemer, our Lord and our God And this which ought to bind us, if it were only by love and gratitude, has another motive more personal to us.

A life of generous penance is to all, even to the most mature, the safer path. Saint Vincent of Paul used to say, "If we had one foot in Heaven, yet if we cease to mortify ourselves, before we could draw the other after it, we should be in danger of losing our soul." Saint Paul says, "All things are lawful to me, but all things are not expedient." There are many things which I might lawfully do which would not help me to overcome my faults or avoid temptations, or sanctify my heart, or save my soul. I am free to enjoy much that is fair, and bright, and sweet, and in itself harmless, but it would not add a grace to my soul, nor a spark of the love of God, nor a fibre of strength, to my will. It would not build me up in the life of God. Now, observe, Saint Paul does not here try those things by the harm they would do him, nor by the danger he might incur. They would do him no good; they would add nothing to his state before God; and they might become occasions of some entanglement and temptation. Therefore he adds, "All things are lawful to me, but I will not be brought under the power of any;" that is, I will keep my liberty by not using it. I will not so use it as to give to anything a power over my peace and tranquillity of heart, or over the freedom of my soul from all things, but Jesus, to whom alone I am in bondage in the sweet service of the spirit of life.

There is need of few words to show how the Sacrament of Penance infuses and perfects this spirit of generous love. For it requires of us a firm resolution of the will against all sin, and it imposes on us a penance in satisfaction for our sins. Now, this penance might be long and rigorous, extending over our whole life; but though it were ever so extended, even until death, it would not make adequate satisfaction for the sins we have committed. How much less adequate reparation to the love of Jesus which we have outraged by commission and omission, by wounds and by coldness.

The practice of the Church in these latter times has been to impose penances which are both light and consoling, such as devotion to the Ever Blessed Trinity, the Sacred Heart of Jesus, the Holy Ghost, or our Blessed Mother – a few prayers to be said once over. Often this is all, and the world mocks at it as a superstition and a nullity; and the pharisaic religion of these latter days treats it as lax and antinomian. "But wisdom is justified by all her children." It is especially the Sacrament of Penance, with these light and benign penances, which awakens the spirit of generous love, and this will do all the rest. It shows us first the price He paid for us – how He suffered for us a Passion equal to, and far beyond, the guilt of all our sins, and of the sins of the whole world. We see, too, how great was the guilt of our sins, which nothing but the most Precious Blood of the Incarnate Son could cancel: how great must be the ingratitude and the hatefulness of our sin, which pierced the Son of God with His unknown and unspeakable sorrows. Every absolution bears this witness to us.

Next it shows us how little He exacts from us. He requires indeed that we should come to Him, that we should leave off sinning, accuse ourselves at His feet, and promise to sin no more. Less than this He could not ask, and no more than this He requires of the greatest sinner. He thereby puts us upon the "law of liberty," of which Saint James writes, "So speak ye, and so do as being to be judged by the law of liberty." He puts us upon probation of our gratitude, generosity, and love. He pardons us at once, even before we fulfil our penance. Our absolution does not depend upon its fulfilment; and the little penance we perform He not only accepts but elevates to a higher order, and invests with a great efficiency. In this way He appeals to our generosity. His own generosity upbraids us. If He be so generous to us, what ought we to be to Him?

And, finally, it inspires by the grace of the Holy Spirit a desire to offer ourselves to Him in reparation. What is past we cannot undo. What remains then but for the future to love Him with generosity, and to give to Him not the fruit only, but the tree with the fruit, that is ourselves, our souls and bodies, to be a "living sacrifice pleasing unto God;" and for this we have many motives. First, because of our sins; next, for the sin of those whom we have tempted: gain, for the sins of all, more especially Christians and Catholics, and finally, for the Passion of Jesus Christ.

Lastly, the spirit of reparation has a great reward, not only in the life to come, but also in this. None are so peaceful, so free, so happy, as the generous. The narrow-hearted are always scrupulous and in bondage to themselves. They have, as Saint Thomas of Villanova says, "Intellectum in coelo, voluntatem in coeno" – they are drawn up by high visions and by the intellectual perception of the blessedness of a devoted and holy life; but they are also drawn down by the soft, alluring, and foolish attachments of taste, custom, fancy, and the fear of the world; and between these two they waver and are distracted, and suffer a perpetual strain like men upon the rack. None are more restless and depressed, than people who take their full liberty in all things which are not sin. They are always wishing for the higher, and falling into the lower, path. They begin with courage to choose the better and the nobler part, and they end in a cowardice which makes them shrink from the least denial of their own will, or limitation of their own liberty. They shrink with fear from an austere life, and yet know that lax lives are always uneasy and unsafe.

Happy are they who can make up their mind. The decided are always calm; even in the midst of trouble they know their path, and their way is clear before them. They who generously choose the higher and more austere life, enter into a great peace. It is sweet, because it is chosen for Jesus' sake. At first, they shrink perhaps from natural infirmity, and the will fears what the light of faith dictates, and what its own choice decides. But the Holy Ghost is a generous Spirit, and never calls a soul to higher paths, without elevating the will freely and generously to choose them. The Cross becomes sweet when it is chosen, and light when it is lifted on the shoulder.

If the life of the generous be happy their death is blessed. The time of their weakness is the time of His power; when they sink under the burden of mortality, then is the hour of His special generosity, and of their ineffable consolation.

And yet, not only in life and death, but, most of all, the reward of the generous is laid up for them in Purgatory. The spirit of reparation gives to their penance a wonderful power of expiation. A few years of loving sorrow, with gratitude and self-chastisement, will expiate we know not what debt of pain. The more penance here the less Purgatory hereafter. Immediately after death Saint Peter of Alcantara was seen ascending with great glory into Heaven, and out of the midst of his joy he said: "See how great a glory a few years of penance bring." Nor is generosity reserved for Saints. Mary Magdalen is the type of generous sorrow. A heroic act not only of martyrdom but of reparation is enough to absolve all guilt and to expiate all pain. In the life of Saint Vincent Ferrer we read of a great and habitual sinner who at last made his confession to him. It was a terrible life of long and complicated wickedness. When the penitent expected long years of mortification and heavy penances, Saint Vincent bade him fast every Friday for a year. The penitent begged him not to trifle with a case so desperate as his, believing that the Saint was speaking in irony. Saint Vincent commuted the penance to the seven penitential psalms.

Once more the penitent begged him not to treat him with levity. The Saint then bade him say once a Pater, Ave, and Gloria. And that night the penitent sinner died, and the Saint saw him in vision ascending to the heavenly glory. The love of God had broken up the fountains of love and sorrow in his heart, and his nature gave way under the compassion of Jesus. The agony of his self-accusation, and the will to expiate, had made a perfect reparation for the sins of a life.

And, lastly, those little privations of a generous love will receive from His hands a great reward. There is no humility and less generosity in saying, "If only I can be saved I shall be content." Our salvation is not the final end of our being, but His glory, and if we aim at being saved at the least glory to our Redeemer, we may easily lose our souls. For what is the greater crown? It is not the visible splendour of the Heavenly Court, but the internal and essential glory of the Saints. It is to be nearer to Him, to know Him more fully, to be more like to Him, and to love Him with a more ardent and eternal love. And this is measured by our state in this life, for glory is but grace made perfect, the fruit of the blossom which now is. This is the thought which, out of the feeble and fearful, has made martyrs, confessors, penitents, missionaries, priests, and nuns. The highest aspirations are often united with the weakest natures. Our natural infirmity shrinks when our will is inflexible. Jesus in His agony is the example of what they have to endure who make satisfaction for sin to God, and He shews us that our suffering does not take away from the perfection of our submission or our sacrifice.

They whom Jesus calls to martyrdom suffer and exult: their lower nature is wounded with ineffable pain, but their higher is in the foretaste of the Beatific Vision. All who have confessed Jesus before men have had to suffer shame and sorrow, but they chose it with gladness for His sake. Penitents have abandoned all that was dearest to them with joy not to be told for the sweetness of making reparation to Him. Sons have left their home and all its charities, dear as life, to expiate, as missionaries among the heathen, the sins of a life not soiled by a mortal sin. Youths have with gladness forsaken the world and all its hopes to take the solitary yoke of Jesus in the sacerdotal life. Daughters, to whom all affections ministered, have turned from all to serve Him in a cloister, or in a rude and exposed life among the souls for which He died; and yet all these have had moments of irresolution and fear, of shrinking, and relapse, in which nothing saved them from falling from their higher aspirations, and losing the vocation of God, but the one deep, still, but constraining thought, sweet and persuasive, that to choose the lot which Jesus chose on earth, would be more pleasing to the Sacred Heart of their Master and their Lord. This one thought of generous love to Him, who has done all for us, for whom we can do nothing, who, nevertheless, accepts the nothing we do, and by working "in us both to will and to accomplish," gives it a power of reparation. This alone has made the earth to blossom like the rose and the lily, and has illuminated the Church with the lights of sanctity, and brought the multitude, whom no man can number, to the throne of Jesus, and to His Eternal joy.

# CHAPTER FIVE

# The Sacrament of Perseverance

Our Divine Lord has said, "He that shall persevere unto the end he shall be saved," which is also to say, and no other shall. Twice He declared this truth in words, which thrill and awe us to read them. "No man putting his hand to the plough, and looking back, is fit for the Kingdom of God" – and again, "Remember Lot's wife." God has revealed to us the history of His elect, running down from the creation through the ages of grace: but all along the line, and beside it, as a parallel, runs the history of those that have fallen. Every state and order of His servants has the witness of instability in itself. Of the Holy Angels created in the nearest likeness of their Maker, and placed upon the steps of the throne of God, multitudes fell into eternal death. Of His elect people, the

Apostle writes, "I would not have you igno-
rant, brethren, that our fathers were all under
the cloud, and all passed through the sea; and
all in Moses were baptized in the cloud and in
the sea; and did all eat the same spiritual food,
and all drank the same spiritual drink (and they
drank of the spiritual rock that followed them,
and the rock was Christ). But with the most of
them God was not well pleased: for they were
overthrown in the desert."

Prophets also have fallen. Balaam, in the
midst of the Divine visitations, perished among
the enemies of God. Seers likewise fell, as
Solomon, wisest of men; and Apostles, as Judas;
and Christians in the first grace of their regeneration, as Ananias and Sapphira. The annals
of the Church are full of such warnings. The
line of heresiarchs is a long history of the forfei-
ture of grace. And in the lives of the Saints the
same examples of perseverance and of falling are
found side by side. In the Franciscan Chroni-
cles, to give one instance for many, we read of a
Brother Justin who renounced the world, high
honours, and great employments, to become a
religious. His progress in the life of perfection
was so great, that he was visited with raptures

in prayer and many supernatural favours. His brethren counted him a saint. He went to Rome in the time of Eugenius IV, who received him with great veneration, would not let him kiss his feet, but embraced him, made him sit at his side, and bestowed many privileges upon him. All this awakened pride, and turned his head. When he went back to his convent Saint John Capistrano said to him: "You went an angel, you are come back a devil." Soon after this he fell into great private sins and open breaches of the public law. He died in prison. These examples teach one truth: all depends on perseverance. Without this nothing avails. The grace, and perfection, and splendour of the angels could not save them.

The election of Israel, the miracles in Egypt, the manna in the wilderness, were all in vain. The converse with God, the resistance of an angel, availed nothing for Balaam. The illumination which laid open the natural and supernatural worlds to Solomon, did not profit him. The daily fellowship with Jesus, His doctrines and miracles, and three years of His presence, did not save Judas. The gift of regeneration and of the Sacraments of grace were all in vain to Ananias and Sapphira. All alike lacked one thing, and that one thing lacking lost them all things. They had not perseverance, and though they had everything else, nothing without this was of any avail.

It remains therefore to show what perseverance is, and how the Sacrament of Penance infuses and sustains it. First, as to the nature of perseverance. Theologians distinguish it into the active and the passive perseverance. The active is a virtue on our part, the passive a gift on the part of God.

The active perseverance consists, first, in our fidelity to the grace God has bestowed upon us, that is, in corresponding with the light of faith in the intellect, with the impulses of charity in the heart, and the inspirations of the Holy Ghost in the will, in surrendering ourselves with a filial and watchful promptness to the operations and calls of God in the soul; secondly, it consists in fervour, which is not so much any ardent affection, or vehement emotion of the heart, as a constant devotion of the will. Fervour is made up of three things, first, regularity in all duties in the order and habit of the interior life; secondly, in punctuality in doing all things in season, at the right time or in the right way; and lastly, exactness in doing all things as perfectly as we can, remembering for whom we do them; and that the greatest actions, if done ill, and without this motive, are as nothing, and that the least actions are great if done perfectly and for God.

And, thirdly, perseverance springs from delicacy of conscience, which consists in the vividness and sensitiveness of the heart, and in the promptness and activity of the will under the operations of grace. The Fathers say, "Res delicata Spiritus Sanctus," because His purity, love, and patience, are grieved even with things of which our dullness makes little account. So I may say a pure conscience has delicate sense derived from the Holy Spirit Himself, and in harmony with all His operations; so that as soon as He moves the conscience answers, as kindred notes vibrate, or as the leaves incline before the motion of the air, and the sea undulates under the presence of the lightest wind.

This is the essence of perseverance on our part, and from this internal state come the acts of obedience, penance, mortification, expiation, reparation, constancy, fortitude, self-sacrifice, and endurance to the end, which constitutes what we call final perseverance.

But it is certain that without the passive perseverance, which is a gift on God's part, no one will so persevere to the end. The Holy Council of Trent teaches that no man without a special privilege of grace will avoid all sin. Not that it is physically impossible, but only morally certain. It is physically possible, that of a thousand arrows shot at a mark every one may strike; but it is morally certain that many will fall short, pass beyond, or swerve aside. There is abstractedly no intrinsic impossibility in this, but it is certain that the wandering of the eye, or the unsteadiness of the hand, or the motions of the air, or the wavering of the will, or some other cause, will hinder the flight and the aim of many in every thousand shafts. So it is in our co-operation with grace. Lights, visitations, inspirations, come down upon us like showers, but it is only a few among many with which we correspond; or if we correspond, it is in an inadequate proportion. We receive grace as a hundred, and we correspond as twenty, or we receive as twenty, and correspond as one. The waste of nature, which is always sowing the world broad-cast, on sea and land, on mountain and rock, with seeds, every one of which has life and fruitfulness in it, is a true analogy to the waste of grace which inundates us, and passes unheeded away.

If, then, there were not another special grace of perseverance by which God, in His free sovereign mercy sustains us, no soul should be saved. And, yet, that grace cannot be merited by us. God has not promised to bestow it on anything we do. There is no proportion, or link established by His promise between our perseverance and this surpassing gift. It is to the end His free and sovereign grace. The first grace and the last, the Alpha and the Omega of our salvation are in His hand alone. No man can merit regeneration, which is the first grace in our salvation: nor the last, without which regeneration is all in vain. God holds the first link and the last of the golden chain of grace in His own hand, and bestows it on whom He will. We may pray for it but we cannot merit it; we may dispose ourselves to receive it, but we can never claim it at His hand. It is bestowed upon us out of pure love and grace, through the prayers and merits of His Saints, out of the Sacred Heart of Jesus, who has purchased it for us in His most Precious Blood.

It is easy then to see how both the virtue and the gift of perseverance is to be lost One mortal sin destroys it utterly. The Prophet Ezechiel warns even the just of their danger of falling: "If the just man turn himself away from his justice, and do iniquity – shall he live? all his justices which he hath done shall not be remembered, in the prevarication by which he hath prevaricated, and in his sin, which he hath committed, in them he shall die." All that he has been, or has done, or has suffered, in one moment is lost. And for such a fall we generally prepare ourselves by a multitude of lesser faults. Satan seldom tempts the just to a mortal sin all at once. The shock of the temptation itself would arouse them to watchfulness. "He that contemneth small things shall fall by little and little." It is by little ruining temptations, which wear and fret away the integrity and firmness of the will, that he begins his assault. He leads men into the occasions of lesser faults, and so by degrees deadens the hatred and the very fear of sin, and inspires a boldness to venture where before they would not have dared to go. Then come strong attractions, fascinations, and entanglements, and last of all the Tempter's hour is come.

And for such a fall he prepares by inspiring a presumption of our own strength. "Contritionem praecedit superbia." Pride goeth before destruction. We confide in our own lights even those which are internal and supernatural, and in our own spiritual attainments as if they were our own. This is what is called the "storm in the harbour," the whirlwind which comes down upon the soul when it has escaped out of the sea into the calm water of the haven, the perdition which falls upon the soul after it has found peace with God, and is anchored to the eternal shore. That which chiefly brings on this great and subtle danger is a secret neglect of prayer, a weariness and aversion from speaking with God, and this again begins in a loss of fervour and punctuality in devotion, and this loss arises from some secret infidelity of the heart which brings films over it and shadows of fear, so that the light and warmth of the Divine Presence is at first slightly veiled as by a mist, and then is hid so that we lose the consciousness of it, and the holy fear which it inspires and keeps alive.

The true cause of those preparatory and secret falls is some interior sin of the heart known only to God and to ourselves. The world has dim eyes and can only see external sins, and even of these only such as blot the life outwardly. But the external act does not constitute the sin. The sin is perfect already in the internal act of the heart by the knowledge of the understanding and the consent of the will. This is the essential malice of sin to which the external act adds only an accidental increase, and the sin of scandal. In this way men prepare themselves long before. It may be for years they stand to all appearance in flower and fruit; but like trees which have a decay at the heart, they go at last in a sudden wind, and all men wonder at their fall till it lays open their heart, and then men wonder that they stood so long and did not come down long ago.

And this shows further how our perseverance is to be sustained. First, and above all, by a habitual consciousness of the love of God, through the Sacred Heart of Jesus working upon our hearts, humbling, softening, and kindling them with love in return. This consciousness that we are objects of the love of God, this sense of a personal relation, and personal friendship with the Sacred Heart of Jesus, is to the soul what the sun, with its ardour and splendour, is to the seeds and to the fruits of the earth. It quickens, vivifies, unfolds, ripens, perfects everything. To doubt of God's love brings winter into the soul; to feel it feebly and faintly is as the cloudy and churlish sky which hinders the ripening influence of the light. In darkness all things pale and die. If only we can live in an habitual sense of our perfect pardon and absolution, through the most Precious Blood of Jesus, of His friendship for us and our discipleship to Him, of His perpetual presence, love, and care, we shall have the root of perseverance firmly fixed in our will, and for this we need no great learning, no mystical, no dogmatical theology. A childlike heart is enough.

Among the martyrs of Cochin China, in these last years, was a simple Catechumen. The heathen scorned him for his ignorance, and mocked him for his inability to answer their objections against the nature of God, and for his obstinacy in dying for a God about whom he could give no account. He answered: "In a family of many children some are grown to mature intelligence, some are growing to youth, some are infants, all love their Father, but all do not know Him equally. The elder can give an account of Him, of His character, and of the reasons why they love Him, but the infants know neither His character nor His name. All that they know is that He is their Father, and that He loves them, and this is their reason for loving Him in return, and trusting Him with all their heart." Such is the true childlike love of God, the basis and the crown of our perseverance.

The next support of our perseverance is a true knowledge of ourselves. There are few more thrilling words in Holy Scripture than these: "There are just men and wise men, and their works are in the hand of God, and yet man knoweth not whether he be worthy of love or hatred." That is, in the searching eyes of God we are so unlike what we are in the twilight of our own, that, whatsoever judgment we may have of ourselves, God may all the while judge of us far otherwise. This salutary fear of deceiving ourselves by too kind an opinion of our own state is the first condition of self-knowledge. Until we are willing to believe that we are probably far more sinful than we have ever known, or suspected, we shall make no great progress in self-knowledge. We have to learn not only our sins but, as we have seen, our personal sinfulness, our unworthiness, our unprofitableness, our littleness, and our weakness.

And this will bring us another support by a growing contrition, ripening into compunction; and this cancels our venial sins, reconciles the heart with God, brings down great grace, and unites the will with the will of Jesus. And from contention springs the spirit of reparation, a generous desire to make atonement to the Sacred Heart which has loved men so much, and has been loved so little. A spirit of reparation draws great graces from the Sacred Heart, and engages all its generosity in our salvation. These four things, love, self-knowledge, contrition, and reparation, with a continual infusion of grace to repair the continual decays of every day, are all we need to sustain this active perseverance on our part. But these four graces are especially those which, as I have shown, the Sacrament of Penance infuses and perfects in us. It is therefore the Sacrament of Perseverance, and the means of preparing ourselves to receive of God the free grace of His Sovereign mercy, the gift of passive perseverance. Such is the outline of the subject I undertook to speak of, and with a few words more I shall conclude. I will then only add four simple rules to obtain this great gift of God.

1. First, use the Sacrament of Penance fully and generously. Pour out your hearts like water. They that so come oftenest to it are the most confirmed in perseverance, and they who are most confirmed in perseverance are they who oftenest come to it. According as we use it, so it will be to us. Happy are they who come month by month, happier they who come week by week. They who come seldom to confession, wonder what others can have to say who come so often. But they who come seldom have always least to say, because they have least self-knowledge. They who come often, as their self-knowledge increases, find a greater facility and a greater desire to come oftener. Many of the Saints, as Saint Charles, confessed every day. We wonder what they could find to accuse themselves of. It was because they were Saints that they saw so much where we see so little. If we had more of the supernatural light of the Sacrament of Penance, we too should see as they did; but to

obtain this spiritual discernment, habitual and frequent confession is necessary.

2. Next, be always beginning. Never think that you can relax, or that you have attained the end. Saint Francis used to say continually to his brothers, "My brethren, let us begin to love God a little." He felt that he was only at the outset of the way of perfection, a mere beginner in the science of God. If we think ourselves to be more, it is because we are less. If we think ourselves more than beginners, it is a sign that we have hardly yet begun. There is no security for perseverance except in always advancing. To stand still is impossible. A boat, ascending a running stream, falls back as soon as it ceases to advance. To hold its place is impossible, unless it gain upon the stream. So in the spiritual life. The past is no guarantee for the future. All the justice of the just man is gone in the day in which he falls, and all his past obedience is no security against present transgression. Our Lord, therefore, warns us to "remember Lot's wife." She was saved by the visitation of Angels, drawn forth from destruction by the constraint of an Angel's hand. She was half-way to safety when she looked back, and was cut off by the

just judgment of God. The past availed nothing. Only present fidelity from moment to moment is security for the future. Therefore, again, our Divine Lord said, "No man putting his hand to the plough and looking back, is fit for the kingdom of God," that is, the husbandman who turns in the furrow to look at his past work, and lingers over his toil, shall never reach the end of the field. What we have done as yet is little compared with what remains to do. We have to perfect our sanctification, which even in Saints is far off. We have to expiate the pains due to a world of sins, surpassing all memory, and as yet we have but little chastised ourselves. We have to complete the chain of graces by which we are bound to the eternal throne, and many links are still wanting. There is no time to lose. Let us hear how an Apostle speaks of perseverance: " Brethren, I do not count myself to have apprehended. But one thing I do: forgetting the things that are behind, and stretching forth myself to those that are before, I press towards the mark, to the prize of the supernal vocation of God in Christ Jesus."

"Know you not that they that run in a race, all run indeed, but one receiveth the prize? So run that you may obtain. And every one that striveth for the mastery, refraineth himself from all things: and they indeed, that they may receive a corruptible crown: but we an incorruptible one. I therefore so run, not as at an uncertainty: I so fight, not as one beating the air: But I chastise my body and bring it into subjection: lest perhaps, when I have preached to others, I myself should become a cast-away."

If Saint Paul had need so to speak, how much more such as we? If all his supernatural grace, his miraculous conversion, and singular vocation, his perils by land and by sea, his labours and fasting, visions and revelations, if in these there was no security that he might not even become a reprobate, how much more cause have we to live and die in holy fear? This then is the second support of perseverance.

3. Thirdly, meditate every day upon the fall of those who begun well. Once perhaps they set out with as fair a hope of eternal life as we have. Their childhood and youth was it may be holier and nearer to God than ours. A bright sunshine and a fair morning gave promise of a noontide of ripeness and an evening of peace. Perhaps they persevered as long, or longer than we have yet,

and that against many dangers and temptations. At last they fell. Their beginning was like ours, and our end may be like theirs. An awful and thrilling truth. It is good to have it always before our eyes. For instance, the fall of the Angels may teach us that no gift, or perfection of grace will avail us if we lack stability. They were created in excellence of knowledge and strength, both natural and supernatural, but they sinned, and what was their sin, but pride of which we have been guilty a thousand times. They desired to be as God; not that they aspired to His immensity, or infinity, or eternity, for the angelic intelligence is too perfect and too luminous for such a folly; but they desired to be independent of God. They contemplated their own proper excellence till they became enamoured by self-love. They sought to be happy in themselves by their own proper and natural beatitude; to suffice to themselves, and to be blissful without God. This was their sin, and what is it but the pride which is the sin of the world, as Saint John calls it, "the pride of life."

We may also meditate on the fall of Judas, whose example is nearer to us than we are wont to imagine. The greatness of his sin deceives many. We believe ourselves to be in no danger of such a guilt, and we forget that the sin of Judas had once a beginning as fair as the sin we may be committing at this hour: and in the end we may fall from God as deliberately as he did. It is a very awful and touching thought that Judas was once an innocent child like as we were; that he was the object of a mother's love, as tender as ever we have known; that perhaps in boyhood he may have lived in the holy fear of the God of Israel more watchfully than ever we lived in the light of the Holy Trinity; the days of his youth were as blameless perhaps as ours; morning and evening came and went, as to us, with their joys and their sorrows, their fears and their hopes of manhood, and the works of life. All that we know is, that he was called to be an Apostle – that he obeyed the call. So far, perhaps, he did more than we have done in corresponding with grace. In this grace he persevered, in the fellowship of Jesus, sharing in His toil and weariness, hunger and thirst, shame and contradiction. He heard His parables, and saw His mighty works of power. What could we have done more? "He having the purse, carried the things that were put therein;" and the sin of covetousness sprang up in him.

But the seeds of it are also in us. His office led him into the occasions of sin. He was tempted, and fell, and should we have stood firm? He was living in the midst of all that ought to have sanctified him, without being sanctified by it.

All without was holy, and ministered grace to him; but within there was a heart-sin which resisted the Holy Ghost; and this spiritual contradiction gradually threw out the habit, and the design, and the daring, by which he fell. He had seen his Master again and again pass unhurt through His enemies. They could lay no hand on Him. He had seen Him do works of mighty power; how could he doubt that He could protect Himself from the Pharisees? What harm to make money where no ill could come? Jesus could protect Himself, and so he sold him for thirty pieces of silver, not doubting, perhaps, that the Priests and the Pharisees were deluding themselves. For we read that "Judas seeing that Jesus was condemned, repented himself." It was a new and unexpected result. He went and made restitution, "casting down the pieces of silver in the temple." He himself confessed that he had sinned in "betraying the innocent blood." Have we done as much in many a fall? And driven to despair at the unforeseen horror, "he went and hanged himself." Judas is an example how a soul once innocent may be slowly changed into the worst sin, and even at last fall with little intention of committing the whole evil which follows from its act. But if the example of Judas be far off from many of us, the fall of Demas is near to us all. We read the pathetic words of Saint Paul: "Demas hath left me loving this world." He was weary of the apostolic life; of journeying by land and by water; of having no fixed dwelling-place, of perils among the heathens, and perils among false brethren, of labours, watchings, and fastings. Why should he be the companion of Apostles? It was a life of counsels; the life of the commandments was enough for such as he. How fair and reasonable all this appears; how like the reasoning and the lives of many at this day. But the Apostle saw deeper. The Holy Ghost reads the heart. Demas "loved this world;" therefore, and for no other reason, he forsook the servants of Jesus Christ, and departed to Thessalonica. Of his end who knows, who can know, till the day when all falls shall be revealed? We shall then know what the Apostle said with tears: "All seek the things that are their own; not the things that are Jesus Christ's."

Let us then meditate often on these things, and remember that falls are not always by the grosser sins which the world takes count of, but by spiritual sins, subtle and secret, which leave no stain upon the outward life, yet are perhaps more deadly because more satanic, that is, more like the fall of angels.

4. And lastly, let no sun go down without praying for the gift of perseverance.

Ask it every day of the Ever-Blessed Trinity: ask it of the Eternal Father, of whom our Divine Lord had said, "No one can snatch them out of the hand of My Father." Ask it of the Eternal Son incarnate, who has said, "All that the Father giveth to Me shall come to Me, and him that cometh to Me I will hot cast out." Ask it also of the Eternal Spirit, the Holy Ghost, for our Lord has also said, "No man can come to me except the Father who hath sent Me draw him." It is by the Holy Ghost which proceedeth from the Father and the Son that Jesus fulfils His promise. "And I, if I be lifted up from the earth, will draw all things to myself." This is the gift of perseverance, the manifold grace of the Ever-Blessed

Trinity encompassing us without and penetrating and sustaining us within, and upholding us above our dangers, and ourselves. Ask it through the prayers of our Blessed Mother, the Mother of God, whose immaculate hands are lifted up day and night before the Sacred Heart of her Son to obtain our salvation; and finally, ask it through the prayers of our guardian Angel, who has kept us from our baptism, in spite of all our infidelities and all the griefs and disappointments we have heaped upon him.

And then onwards and upwards. Onwards against the resistance, both within and without, which hinders our advance in the life of God. Onwards without fear, or doubt, or wavering. And upwards, aiming as high as we can, for we have to ascend the mountains of the Lord's House, which are exalted very high. We have three mountains to scale before we see the Vision of Peace. The first is Mount Calvary, by the way of the Cross, in penance, mortification, and self-denial, sharp indeed, but sweet when we remember our sins and the love of Jesus. For this end I have endeavoured to speak of the Sacrament of Penance as an object of love, that souls may be drawn to it as their true rest, refreshment, and consolation. The second is Mount Thabor, the mountain of the Beatitudes, in which Jesus reveals Himself to hearts purified on Calvary, that is, in the Sacrament of the Altar, in which Jesus stands surrounded by the meek, the merciful, the clean of heart, the persecuted for justice sake, blessing and changing them into His own likeness. And the last mountain is Mount Sion, upon which is the Holy City and the vision of God. To this we are called. Jesus is ever saying, "Come up hither," ever promising to us a crown of perseverance. A few short years, and a little sorrow, and a few conflicts, and perhaps some falls and a generous repentance, with a loving reparation, then comes the end, eternal rest and the vision of Beauty and of Peace. "He that shall overcome shall thus be clothed in white garments, and I will not blot out his name out of the Book of Life, and I will confess his name before My Father and before His Angels." He that shall overcome, I will make him a pillar in the temple of my God: and he shall go out no more, and I will write upon him the name of my God, and the name of the city of my God, the new Jerusalem which cometh down out of Heaven from my God, and my new name." "To

him that shall overcome, I will give to sit, with
Me in My throne, as I also have overcome, and
am set down with My father in His throne."

www.ingramcontent.com/pod-product-compliance
Lightning Source LLC
Chambersburg PA
CBHW020740130626
46554CB00006B/2072